W9-BDH-738

NATURE STUDIES

Sustenance 92
> Sustenance 92 (detail)

NEETA MADAHAR NATURE STUDIES

With essays by *Carlo McCormick* and *David Chandler*

A PHOTOWORKS PUBLICATION

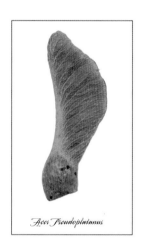

Acer Pseudoplatanus

FOREWORD
AND ACKNOWLEDGEMENTS

NATURE STUDIES IS THE FIRST PUBLICATION DEVOTED TO THE WORK OF BRITISH ARTIST NEETA MADAHAR. IT FOCUSES ON TWO RECENT WORKS: THE FIRST, A SERIES OF FIFTEEN COLOUR PHOTOGRAPHS CALLED *Sustenance*, WAS MADE IN 2003; THE OTHER, ENTITLED *Falling*, IS A NEW WORK THAT COMPRISES A VIDEO AND FIVE STILL PHOTOGRAPHS.

Although very different in form, both *Sustenance* and *Falling* are thematically related and, in part, this book attempts to draw out those connections and suggest the wider concerns of an important emerging artist. Both works are a response to nature and embody the direct observation of and intimate, everyday contact with the natural world. But both works also suggest a constructed rather than spontaneous heart to those intimate moments of wonder. *Sustenance* and *Falling* are finely balanced on a sense of artificiality, on a heightened sense of drama and even fantasy in commonplace situations. It is this detachment, or odd counterpoint to reality that also releases and enriches the works. They resist categorisation, matching something naïve and childlike in their vision to a knowing sophistication that has strong echoes of Surrealism, and that also hints at something darker, more threatening, around and above us.

The texts in this book, by Carlo McCormick on *Sustenance* (an essay first published in the American magazine Aperture) and my own, elaborate on these ideas, suggesting some of the artistic, cultural and historical resonances of Madahar's work.

Falling has been made as the result of a collaborative three-way commission by Fabrica, Photoworks and inIVA (Institute of International Visual Arts), and this book is published to coincide with the first complete showing of the work at Fabrica in Brighton during October and November of 2005. Many people from those organisations, and others, have been involved in the commission, exhibition and publication and we would like to thank them for all their help and advice. In particular, our thanks go to Tom Ward and Peter Forsyth of Sandstorm, who were responsible for the video animation and have generously supported the DVD production for this publication, to Miguel d'Oliveira for creating the animation soundtrack and the Arts Council England, whose continuing support of Photoworks has enabled this publication to be produced. Special thanks also go to Daniel Wilson (who co-ordinated the exhibition), Matthew Miller and all the staff of Fabrica; to Cylena Simonds and all the staff of inIVA; to Gilane Tawadros, formerly Director of inIVA, who was instrumental in bringing Neeta's original proposal to our attention; to Rebecca Hicks and all at Purdy Hicks; to my colleagues at Photoworks, Rebecca Drew, Gordon MacDonald, Ben Burbridge and Polly Carter, for their constant help and support; to Dean Pavitt of LOUP for his beautiful and sensitive design; to Carlo McCormick for allowing us to use his excellent essay and to *Aperture* for allowing us to reproduce it; and lastly we offer our sincere thanks to Neeta Madahar, who has shown an admirable combination of inspiration and professionalism, as well as boundless energy, throughout the various stages of this project.

David Chandler
Director, Photoworks

Sustenance 104
(detail)

Sustenance

Sustenance 48

NEETA MADAHAR NATURE STUDIES

Sustenance 104

Sustenance 51

NEETA MADAHAR NATURE STUDIES

Sustenance 114

NEETA MADAHAR'S ORNITHOLOGY
Carlo McCormick

WHAT WE SEE ARE THOSE GLIMPSES OF LIFE THAT ARE RELEGATED, BY NATURE ITSELF, TO THE PERIPHERAL GAZE, THOSE EPISODIC ENCOUNTERS WITH THE QUOTIDIAN. NEETA MADAHAR'S STUNNING FIFTEEN-IMAGE SERIES *Sustenance* FRAMES SUCH CASUAL SIGHTINGS AS A BIRD IN A BACKYARD AS PRECIOUS, DEFINING MOMENTS.

What she captures is more than a mere pose within the fleeting: it is a rich, contemplative stillness; a chance for both artist and viewer to look, with mesmeric clarity of detail, at the avian community whose constant cohabitation with humans has rendered their presence ostensibly incidental. Birds are the subjects of these photographs, but hardly the sum of their content. It is not that we get to see what she sees – in fact, the artist hides from her subjects behind closed blinds, only sensing the right moment to photograph by peering through the blinds or from the familiarity of a bird's song – what we share with Madahar here is a sense of *wonder*.

Born of an Indian family who came to England in the 1960s, Madahar earned her degree in mathematics (a familial requisite), before coming to the understanding that she was an artist. She studied fine art at Winchester School of Art, working most often with video, and then moved to the US, to Boston, to take her masters degree. It was during this time, living outside the city, that she began making pictures of these birds – which are something of a novelty in England, where an American cardinal or a bluejay carries a degree of exotic cachet – setting up her camera for a period of eighteen months on the balcony of her apartment.

Perhaps it is that play of distance that suggests a personal connection within this work. India, England, the United States – not really a far-flung cultural mix in this age of curatorial globalism: Madahar certainly understands the paths and pollinations of migration. In fact, her earliest photographs (she first picked up a camera in her thirties) were all about that hypothetical construct we call *home*. 'People would ask me where I'm from,' she remembers, 'so for me it became a question of where is home.' It is a word rich with ambiguity – be it about her race, her parents' home, or what part of town she was living in. That location, at once physical and metaphysical, is the site where we enjoy watching this bit of the animal kingdom at its birdhouses, feeders, and baths. The shift in attention is not so far from the pictures of Madahar's parents' home or her American apartment; it's just a few steps, after all, from the domestic interior to the balcony.

There is much slippage here between viewer and subject: the artist's eye that does not see but approximates by sound and time of day; the mass of images distilled down to this essence; the element of chance that would make John Cage proud; the formality of a decisive moment that would impress Cartier-Bresson; that elusive topography where nature and humanity collide. Madahar charts a pleasure that is feral, unpredictable, yet eminently of the leisure time and comforts of suburban sensibilities. She works at the intersection where we have access to the wild: the domestic site *within* nature. Of course, the frame is elemental to this fiction. We do not see that just beyond its borders are a parking lot, a sprawl of malls and meaninglessness. Madahar's journey from the living room to a collective fantasy of the wilderness does not, however, trace a fault line between civilization and the idyll; it is, rather, the *axis* upon which her discourse on this disjunction revolves.

Perhaps the oddest question raised by this eccentric set of pictures is whether they are nature-photography or portraiture. This is most definitely not a contemplation of the sublime (such as those left us by great wilderness photographers), nor is it picturesquely pastoral. These are pictures of birds that have been seduced into our world by a codependent system: they want an easy meal, and we want them to fill up the void of our loneliness. (I suppose many of us are strange old folks sitting on a park bench and throwing breadcrumbs to the pigeons when it comes to communing with art or nature.) The more we look at them, the more truly wonderful they are. Self-evident in these profoundly ambiguous photographs is their startling degree of anthropomorphism. Madahar says that birds are 'so similar to us in the way they feed and socialize, in their patterns of behaviour, that they became perfect symbols... as a natural extension of ourselves.' Here, then, the particularity of environment (birds, for all their travels, do belong to a specific region) is subject to a more poetic sense of universality.

Whenever the fluidity of nature is broken, when it is stilled by some aesthetic intervention, the result has the quality of a *memento mori*. Cessation is the ultimate contemplation of what is alive as an artifact of mortality. The way we halt this inevitability is a subject central to Madahar's work. There is a perfection here that is disturbing, a quiet so disquieting that the suspended moment hardly seems real. Think of flowers that are so perfect and vibrant that we assume they must be fake and you get a sense of Madahar's birds. This is the illustrative voice, drawn from the seventeenth-century English naturalist philosophers, who would travel the world to collect its myriad flora and fauna or meditate upon their own backyards to divine the secret order of the universe (later conjured on American shores by John James Audubon, Martin Johnson Heade and Henry Thoreau).

This sense of artifice was not an end that Madahar strove for, but 'a delight' when it came through. Before she embarked on this series, in fact, it was her aspiration to work with dioramas like those encountered in natural-history museums. 'Just as the naturalists were intent on ways to categorize, classify, and understand nature,' the artist explains, 'dioramas are used as an educational tool to make sense of history. I love their compression of time and geography.' For Madahar, who chooses to print her photographs digitally on Somerset Velvet paper — most commonly associated with watercolours — the digital is subservient to the conventional means of fine art photography. Although they are difficult to believe, these images use no collage, montage, or visual manipulation. By making evident our wonderment, by finding the extraordinary in the ordinary, Madahar wraps together the whole question of truth and beauty that, as much as ever, remains an argument on the nature of veracity in photography.

NEETA MADAHAR NATURE STUDIES

Sustenance 79

Sustenance 101

Falling

THE SKY IS FALLING
David Chandler

THINGS FALL FROM THE SKY: RAIN FALLS, SNOW FALLS, NIGHT FALLS, BOMBS FALL. AND IN OUR DREAMS, LIKE ICARUS, WE FALL; FALLING INTO NOTHING, INTO OBLIVION.
And what if the sky itself falls? In popular myths and fairytales the falling sky is a common figure for irrational or unnecessary fears, and yet its transformational images — of air become solid, of gravity become heavy matter, of space itself collapsing upon us — are potent and enduring symbols of the ultimate apocalypse. This potency remains perhaps because the idea of staring up at the sky weaves myth and reality together. Arching across civilisations the sky has been mapped and studied for guidance (both emotional and physical), for signs of salvation and for portents of the future, but this has coexisted with another kind of watching, one tied to everyday dependencies and very real threats of natural and man-made disaster. As an image of infinite space, of freedom and hope the sky also represents uncertain destinies and holds the spectre of uncontrollable destructive power; it is both the beginning and the end.

Falling
(video still)

Neeta Madahar's new video and photographic work *Falling* touches on these broad mythic associations, and yet they are framed in a way that, at first sight, presents something very simple, innocent and child-like. The video animation for *Falling* unfolds as a languorous dream, a visual balm of gently spinning sycamore seeds falling from a blue, cloud-scattered sky. Madahar's idea for the work was to reconstruct personal childhood memories of playing with the 'helicopter' seeds as part of a new imaginary space, and in the process expand those memories into a new temporal experience in which the fleeting moment, that element of playful excitement — so difficult to grasp and remember — becomes an extended and extravagantly detailed reverie. In *Falling* the child's thrill at nature's trick, one that works more or less every time, becomes a slow meditation on the state of wonder itself and on the delicate balance struck between gravity and nature's own plan to resist it; the small-scale marvel becomes something more symphonic.

As the seeds of *Falling* turn their way through time, and as they appear to come closer and closer to the viewer, they suggest different journeys and transitions, from one place and from one state to another. *Falling*, for example, might be seen as a metaphor for migration and the idea of journeys open to chance and to random patterns of settlement and growth. Although there would be an obvious connection to Madahar's cultural background in this (she was born in England from Indian parents who arrived here in the 1960s), in *Falling* she is more interested in the personal journeys that might be suggested by wind blown seeds. The film suggests her excitement at the idea of drifting, of a chance taken; at the sense of possibility in moving from place to place and approaching unknown horizons. And, while the still photograph *Landed* appears to bring a sense of resolution to those journeys, the stream in this image is another hint of restlessness and movement, as the water carries away its share of seeds it suggests different journeys and different narratives intertwined.

But the implied journeys in *Falling* are not just cultural and geographic. As the falling seeds are rendered in ever-greater detail, we are reminded that the child's playful sense of wonder is changed with education into a different kind of curiosity. As the flight patterns of sycamore seeds become the basis of science-class experiments, and nature's magic takes on a more rational character, seeing also shifts into observation. We might notice, for example, if we watch closely enough, that one of the falling seeds is split in two allowing quiet notes of imperfection and difference to creep into the picture. We are encouraged to look and learn in the great tradition of nature study, where examining and recording has its own kind of wonder, an obsessive almost guilty pleasure.

Madahar has spoken of her work dealing with 'our need to meet nature on our own terms' and both *Falling* and the other work in this book, *Sustenance*, connect with the comforting thought, again so familiar from the classroom, that nature's wonders can be found close to home, and that our imaginative responses to them might begin here too. But, although born in this domestic context, both works revel in its strangeness; suburban nature studies are heightened into a kind of surreal drama, in which our spatial coordinates are confused and things – still and moving – seem artificial, transmuted into a glowing hyperreality. If the *Sustenance* photographs remind us of dioramas (those birds are too perfect for life), then the status of the digitally recast seeds in *Falling* is similarly uncertain. Their spiralling motion is too mechanical, it is mesmerically wrong, and their represented form – indeterminate images somewhere between coloured drawing and photograph – becomes almost grotesque in its unwavering precision and distorted scale as the seeds reach the foreground and drift beyond the frame.

So, if the seed fall begins in wonderment it ends, like confetti showers and ticker-tape parades, in a kind of delirium. For Madahar, an important element of her film's restaging of memory was that it should be a physical as well as a visual experience, that we should imagine these sycamore seeds falling around us and brushing against our face. She enjoys the ambiguity of this implied sensation; pleasure and a sense of abandon tinged with discomfort and loss of control. Excitement and anxiety, as Freud noted about 'typical' dreams such as those of flying and falling, are closely related, and Madahar's film draws on that tension.

However, if we are increasingly keen to link extraordinary dreams to commonplace experiences and in a sense to de-fuse them, if the self-styled 'dream doctors' of the internet happily attribute falling dreams to a simple lack of stability in our lives, then *Falling* surely alludes to something else in

the irresistible downward pull of gravity, to something deeper that taps into another, larger-scale reservoir of human fear and anxiety about falling through time and space. Although the reference is not specific, Madahar admits that something of the events of 9/11 2001 in the US have left a trace in her film. The epic tragedy and mind-numbing horror of the attacks on New York in particular took its most terrible form in those desperate figures of people driven to jump from the 'twin towers' to their deaths. In these images our deepest insecurities about the strange disjunctions of scale that underpin the fabric of our world were chillingly played out, the assurances of technology and progress evaporating into a sickeningly visceral waking dream. All that is left is the body, alone, with an unthinkable velocity losing consciousness and humanity as it is pulled inexorably towards the end.

It is not surprising that the photographs and video clips of this appalling sight have since become taboo in the media and elsewhere, a kind of pornography. Respect for the deceased would be a good enough reason for this, but the thought lingers that we may also be too close to these images' sense of deep trauma, that it is perhaps their eerie familiarity from our worst imaginings that has made them intolerable and that has, in turn, helped to suppress them.

These disturbing psychological connections are difficult to contemplate, and potentially overwhelming for a work of art with many resonances, but the anthropomorphism of Madahar's work, already noted by Carlo McCormick in relation to *Sustenance, is* powerfully present in *Falling*. It is significant that in the main sequence of her film Madahar's sycamore seeds do not fall from a tree but appear, initially as an indistinct visitation of black shapes, from nowhere, straight out of the sky. In this subtle narrative ploy the universality of the film is established. *Falling* spans time; not just the extended moment of its reverie but in its intimations of birth, life and death and in its profoundly elegiac scattering of souls.

Falling 2
> Falling 3
>> Falling 4

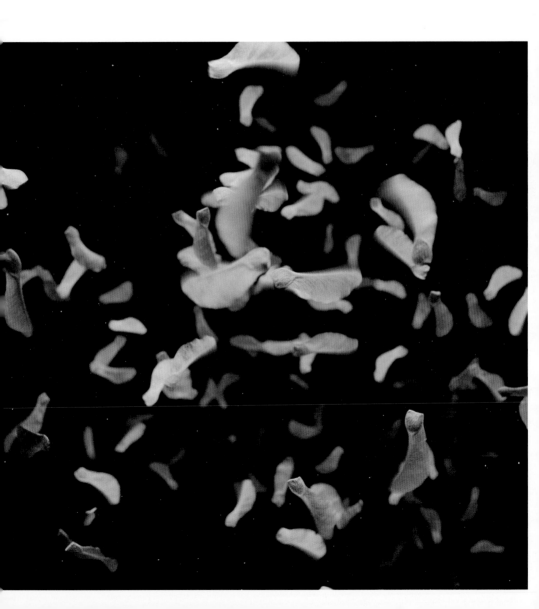

Landed

NEETA MADAHAR NATURE STUDIES

Falling (video stills)

Neeta Madahar: *Nature Studies* is
published by Photoworks to coincide with
an exhibition of *Falling* at Fabrica, Brighton
from 8 October to 6 November 2005

Falling is jointly commissioned by
Fabrica, Photoworks and inIVA (the
Institute of International Visual Arts)

Edited by David Chandler
Designed by LOUP
Printed in Great Britain by Dexter Graphics Ltd

Carlo McCormick's essay is reproduced
with the kind permission of Aperture. It first
appeared in Aperture 179, Summer 2005.

British Library Cataloguing-in-Publication Data
A catalogue record for this book is
available from the British Library.

ISBN 1-903796-16-4

Distributed by Cornerhouse Publications
70 Oxford Street, Manchester, M1 5NH
T: 0161 200 1503
F: 0161 200 1504
E: publications@cornerhouse.org

Photoworks is an independent arts organisation
that brings an international perspective to
promoting photography in the South East of
England. Photoworks operates over four main
areas of activity: commissioning new work,
producing exhibitions, publishing books and
a twice-yearly magazine, and developing
the audience for photography through
education and participation programmes.

Nature Studies is published with the support
of Arts Council England and Sandstorm.
Fabrica's role in the commissioning and exhibiting
of *Falling* is part-financed by the European Union.

Biography
Neeta Madahar graduated with an MFA in Studio
Art from the School of the Museum of Fine Arts and
Tufts University in Boston, USA in 2003 and with
a BA in Fine Art from Winchester School of Art and
Southampton University in 1999. She has exhibited her
work internationally, including the Rencontres d'Arles
Photography Festival in France, 2004, and the Institute
of International Visual Arts in London, 2005. Her work
is in several private and public collections, including
the Victoria and Albert Museum, London and the Fogg
Art Museum, Harvard University, Massachusetts. She
is represented by Howard Yezerski Gallery in Boston,
USA and Purdy Hicks Gallery in London, England.

Artist's Acknowledgments
In addition to the individuals and organisations
mentioned in the foreword, Neeta Madahar would
also like to thank the following for their help in
the production of *Falling*: Dr. David Boyd and
Newbury Amateur Astronomical Society, Barbara
Bosworth, Anne-Marie Francis, Paul Hemingway,
Richard Pinches, Christina Seely, Rosemary Shirley,
Youngsuk Suh and Spectrum Photographic.